1. Jack Gleeson had said that Joaquin Phoenix's portrayal of Commodus in *Gladiator* was a major influence in the way he played Joffrey.

2. Many of the scenes in the last episode of each season of Game of Thrones actually occur in the early chapters of the following book. This is because they ran out of content for the first season and had to tap into the second book for additional scenes.

3. The actress who played Sansa Stark adopted her "dire wolf" Lady after she grew too big and was replaced by computer graphics.

4. Cersei never gave birth to a natural child of Robert Baratheon. She was only pregnant with his child once, but she had it aborted.

5. Each episode of the TV series costs (on average) just over $6,000,000 USD to create.

6. In the books it is Sandor Clegane who tells Sansa how he was wounded as a child, but in the TV show it is Littlefinger.

7. In the final episode of season 1, when Joffrey brings Sansa to see her father's head on a spike, if you look closely you can see that one of the heads is a replica of the former American president, George W. Bush. The creators were forced to apologize and the President's head was digitally removed when the show was released online.

8. The first time we see Tywin Lannister on screen he is skinning a stag. The stag is the sigil of the Baratheon House. The actor practiced for this scene by spending time with a hunting instructor who taught him how to skin a real stag.

9. Since the TV series began, thousands of baby girls have been named Khaleesi, despite that being a title and not a name.

10. In the books, Ned Stark falls off his horse and breaks his leg. In the TV series he is stabbed with a spear by a Lannister soldier.

11. Pouring molten gold onto someone's head or down their throats was a favorite punishment of Genghis Khan and the Mongol Empire, which the Dothraki horse-lords were based off of.

12. A real stag that had been hit by a car was used for the scene where the Starks discover the dire wolf pups. According to the crew the stag had been rotting for two days and the smell was disgusting.

13. In the books there are 300 members of the Night's Watch. In the TV show there are 400.

14. No real wolves were used in the making of Game of Thrones because wolves as pets or actors is illegal in the United Kingdom.

15. The character Talisa does not appear in the books. She replaced Jeyne Westerling. This has been regarded as the largest divergence from the plot of books, as Jeyne Westerling was not present at the Red Wedding.

16. Arya Stark and Tywin Lannister never meet or exchange words in the books. In the TV show they share several scenes when she becomes his cup-bearer. In the books she was Roose Bolton's cup-bearer.

17. In America, Arya was in the top 10 baby names for girls in 2012.

18. In the TV series, Arya Stark did not change costumes between season 2 and 5.

19. In the TV show, Jamie Lannister says he stabbed the Mad King, but in the books he said he slit his throat.

20. The giant Wun Wun's full name is Wun Weg Wun Dar Wun.

21. Osha and Theon never have sexual relations in the books.

22. Economists in Northern Ireland have stated that the Game of Thrones series has boosted their economy by more than $100,000,000.

23. In the books it is only suggested that Stannis has sex with Melisandre but in the TV show it happens on screen.

24. The battle tapestries seen hanging in various places (like Stannis or Renly's tent) in the TV show depict real English battles. Most often the Battle of Hastings.

25. In the books, the first person Arya has Jaqen H'ghar kill for her is Chiswyck, not The Tickler.

26. Arya's kill list is much longer in the books than the TV show. The complete list is: Amory Lorch, Cersei Lannister, Chiswyck, Dunsen, Gregor Clegane, Ilyn Payne, Joffrey Baratheon, Meryn Trant, Polliver, Raff the Sweetling, Sandor Clegane, The Tickler, and Weese.

27. The first episode of the series aired on the real life birthday of Sean Bean (Ned Stark)

28. Lena Headley (Cercei) was pregnant during the filming of season 1 and her baby bump can be seen in several scenes.

29. The only time in the *entire* series that the whole Stark family is gathered together is when they greet Robert Baratheon as he and his entourage arrives in Winterfell.

30. Valyrian steel and obsidian (dragonglass) are the only two things that can harm the White Walkers.

31. The actor who plays the chief pyromancer (Roy Dotrice) is also the narrator of the Game of Thrones audiobooks.

32. George RR Martin has said that the Sparrows are based on the real life Catholic Church when they went through the Protestant Reformation.

33. The actor who plays Aemon Targaryen in the TV series is legally blind, just like his character.

34. The official words of House Lannister are: "Hear me roar." This is often confused with the common saying: "A Lannister always pays his debts."

35. The Game of Thrones TV series has only used six different writers to create their screenplays. Most HBO shows use an average of 20.

36. In the books Cersei never slaps or spanks Joffrey.

37. In the books it was Ser Jacelyn Bywater who replaced Janos Slynt as commander of City Watch. Not Bronn.

38. In the book, Davos' left hand is mutilated by Stannis as a punishment for smuggling. In the show, it's his right hand.

39. The scene where Sansa is almost raped during the riot at King's Landing was written specifically for the TV show.

40. The actress who plays Shae has starred in several hardcore German adult films.

41. The characters in Game of Thrones were inspired by George RR Martin's pet turtles from his childhood. They kept dying and he imagined they were killing each other off.

42. In the books, Renly's throat was cut by the shadow monster, not stabbed in the back.

43. "Here we stand," are the official words of House Mormont. Jorah Mormont's TV dialogue has several lines that are a variation of those words.

44. In the books, Renly's personal guard is called the Rainbow Guard. In the TV show it was changed to Renly's Kingsguard because of issues with the LGBT community.

45. Jamie Lannister doesn't have a reading disability in the books.

46. Dire wolves were a real species of wolf that are now extinct. They are estimated by biologists to have been about 20-30% large than the grey wolf.

47. In the TV show, Daenerys and Khal Drogo's first sex scene is portrayed as somewhat non-consensual. In the book, the sex is totally consensual and it is Daenerys that takes the lead.

48. In the books it is only implied through rumor and innuendo that Renly is a homosexual. It the TV series it is shown on-screen multiple times.

49. The premiere episode of Season 4 had so many viewers it crashed HBO Go and blew up the record set by The Sopranos series finale.

50. The character Alton Lannister was created specifically for the TV show. He was the Lannister sent to King's Landing to deliver Robb's demands.

51. The Night Watch oath is different in the TV show than the books. In the show the following line is missing: "I am the fire that burns against the cold, the light that brings the dawn, the horn that wakes the sleepers."

52. Irri was killed off in the TV show because the actress who portrayed her could not get an extension on her EU work visa.

53. In the books it is Jeyne Poole who is forced to marry Ramsay Bolton.

54. The famous pop singer, Lily Allen was originally cast to play Yara Greyjoy, but then she found out about the scene where Theon fondles her (unbeknownst that Yara is his sister) and she dropped out of the project.

55. All major plot points (including the ending of the show) has been revealed to the Game of Thrones producers. George RR Martin was worried that he might die like Robert Jordan, and someone else would have to finish his work.

56. Game of Thrones is the most pirated TV show in television/torrent history. HBO doesn't have a problem with that. CEO Richard Plepler said it was "Terrific marketing."

57. The Mountain has three black dogs on his shield in the books. In the TV series there is only one black dog.

58. In the books Sansa was not aware she was to marry Tyrion until five minutes before the start of the wedding.

59. The white ravens seen in the TV show had to be imported (at great cost) from Germany. It would have been much cheaper to get one from Canada but international regulations prohibit importing white ravens to Europe.

60. Old Nan was written out of the TV show because the actresses who played her died of old age. They were going to replace her with a new actress but decided not to out of respect for the dead.

61. The Hound has a deep hatred for Tyrion but it is never revealed why.

62. Tommen Baratheon is portrayed by three different child actors in the TV series.

63. NATO member, Turkey, has banned its military members from watching Game of Thrones because they believe it will corrupt them.

64. Keisha Castle-Hughes (Obara Sand) was the first Oscar-nominated actress to star in Game of Thrones.

65. George RR Martin once lost a football bet and had to add a character into the books whose house sigil resembled the Dallas Cowboys logo. The character was Ser Patrek of King's Mountain and in the story he was killed by Wun Wun the giant. (New York Giants, get it?)

66. It isn't revealed until the third book that Joffrey sent the assassin to kill Bran.

67. George RR Martin said Lord of the Rings was unrealistic because of the lack of priests and religion.

68. In the books there is no character named Guymon. He was written into the TV show and named after executive producer Guymon Casady.

69. In the books, Amory Lorch was not killed by Jaqen H'ghar. He was tossed into the bear pit and eaten by the bear.

70. Valyrian steel is based off Damascus steel. Both super-strong and both techniques lost to the ages.

71. Jamie Lannister never kills a fellow Lannister in the books, but in the TV show he kills several.

72. George RR Martin was not involved in the creation of the Dothraki language.

73. The producers filmed a death scene with Jon Arryn and Cersei Lannister but it was cut from the episode. In the scene, Jon Arryn fell out of bed dying of poison. He grabs a letter and starts writing frantically but Cersei appears and stomps on his fingers. They share a look and then he dies.

74. In the TV show, Catelyn tells Roose Bolton she didn't have a bedding ceremony because Eddard didn't want one. In the books, it Is made clear there definitely was one. When a producer was asked if it was changed or she was lying, he gave a vague answer.

75. In the books, Missandei is around 10-years-old. In the TV series she is closer to 25. Thus in the book there is no relationship between her and Grey Worm.

76. In the books, the Battle of Blackwater takes place during the day. In the TV show it takes place at night.

77. The costumes used in the TV show are worn every day for two weeks before being used on screen. This gives them a more realistic look since they become covered in dirt and grime.

78. In the online credits, HBO accidently listed the leader of the White Walkers as Night's King, but it was quickly removed. George RR Martin has said this was an error and not a spoiler.

79. Jaime and Bronn never travelled to Dorne in the books. That was Balon Swann. His plot line was cannibalized. This was because Balon Swann was a minor character and the scenes would take up too much time for a minor character.

80. Jaime Lannister received his knighthood as a battlefield commission after the last fight in the campaign against the Kingswood Brotherhood. He was knighted by Ser Arthur Dayne.

81. In the books Lysa Arryn's son is Robert but in the TV series it was changed to Robin so the audience wouldn't be confused.

82. George RR Martin has said the Iron Throne is about 100x larger ("Made up of thousands of swords) in the books than in the TV series.

83. The character called The Spice King does not appear any time in the books.

84. Peter Dinklage (Tyrion) is the highest-paid actor on the TV series. He is also the highest paid dwarf in the acting business.

85. The scene where Ramsay sexually assaults Sansa actually happens to Jeyne Poole in the books and the scene is much more brutal.

86. George RR Martin has stated that Game of Thrones takes place on Earth but in an alternate reality.

87. Strong Belwas and Arstan Whitebeard were omitted from the third season of Game of Thrones. The reason was it was not realistic for Barristan Selmy to hide his identify from the audience.

88. Strong Belwas' history and backstory was merged with Daario.

89. The actor who played Daario was changed between season 3 and 4 because the actor wanted more money.

90. In the TV show, Sansa picks up a feather from the stone floor in the crypt at Winterfell. This is the same prop feather that was placed there in season 1 episode 1 by Robert Baratheon.

91. Jaqen H'ghar did not help Arya escape Harrenhal. She did it with the help of her friends, Gendry and Hot Pie.

92. The Sons of the Harpy are only supposed to attack at nighttime. Never during the day. But in the show there are many daytime attacks.

93. In the first draft of the screenplay, Arya worked as a peddler in Braavos (like in the books) but it was decided to be too boring.

94. George RR Martin got a lot of death threats after the TV episode of the Red Wedding aired. That episode is also the only episode in the series not to have a song playing during the credits.

95. In the books, Jamie Lannister was a squire for Sumner Crakehall, not Barristan Selmy.

96. In the ninth episode of season 1, a Wilhelm Scream can be heard after Tyrion wakes up from being knocked into the head during a battle.

97. Tyrion is the only character in the Game of Thrones world that meets both Aemon and Daenerys Targaryen.

98. Margaery Tyrell was aware of the plan to poison Joffrey. In the TV series however she is surprised when Olenna admits that it was her. In the books, Margaery was part of the conspiracy.

99. In the TV series, Brienne ends up with The Hound's horse (Stranger) but only The Hound is supposed to be able to control the horse. It bites everyone else.

100. Several prominent musicians (including the drummer for Coldplay, Will Champion) can be seen playing instruments in the Red Wedding scene.

101. The fake heart that Daenerys eats in season one was so messy and so sticky that ended up getting stuck to a toilet.

102. In the TV series, Gendry's story line is combined with Edric Storm. In the books Gendry never meets Melisandre.

103. In the books, the dire wolves are over six-feet-tall when standing on four legs. In the books they are only about 4-feet-tall.

104. Aemon Targaryen is the only character to die on-screen of natural causes.

105. Gandalf's famous sword (Glamdring) is one of the hundreds of fake swords that make up the Iron Throne prop in the TV show.

106. Ser Barristan Selmy does not die in the books.

107. The first four episodes of season 5 were leaked online before the first episode aired on HBO. In less than hour, each episode was downloaded more than 120,000 times.

108. Tywin Lannister was 67-years-old when he died.

109. Lena Headey's (Cercei) nude scene in season 5 was shot with a body double. This is because she was pregnant. The actress whose breasts you see is Rebecca Van Cleave.

110. The Meeren riots did not happen in the book and Daenerys never had anyone publically executed.

111. The scenes with the bear were shot in Los Angeles because it was prohibited to transport the bear to the United Kingdom. Why didn't they just find another bear? Well there only a few bears alive that are trained to work with actors and none of them live in the UK.

112. After Bran escapes Winterfell and heads north, he passes by Hadrian's Wall, a stone structure that The Wall from the books was based on.

113. Bronn is never poisoned in the books.

114. The writers of the TV series have inserted numerous fake death scenes into the screenplays as practical jokes on the actors.

115. In the books, Tyrion's face is greatly disfigured and most of his nose is chopped off. In the TV show he escapes the Battle of Blackwater with barely a scratch. When Cersei sees him in the show, she says: "They said you'd lost your nose, but it's not as gruesome as all that."

116. In the TV series, the Stormcrows were folded into the mercenary company the Second Sons. This was done purely as a cost-saving measure as they didn't want to spend more money on additional costumes and actors.

117. It is not revealed in the books who shot Ygritte with the arrow.

118. In the TV series, Thoros and Melisandre have several conversations in High Valyrian and this language was created specifically for the show.

119. Ros the prostitute was written in the TV show to have a much larger role than the books. She replaced at least three other characters.

120. The actor (Ian Whyte) who played The Mountain in season 2, also plays the giant Wun Wun in season 5.

121. It is never revealed exactly what happened to Syrio Forel but George RR Martin has hinted in interviews that he might still be alive.

122. The first episode of season 5 was aired simultaneously worldwide. It began at 6PM PST.

123. The moon door wasn't a giant hole in the floor in the books. It was just like a normal door on the wall.

124. Episode 9 and 10 from season 4 were converted to the IMAX format and shown in select theaters in 2014.

125. The TV episode where Tyrion Lannister killed his father (Tywin Lannister) was originally aired on Father's Day.

126. There is only one flashback scene in the TV show.

127. Readers of the books were not completely convinced that Ramsay Bolton had castrated Theon. The TV show made it much more clear.

128. In the books, it is not Mance Rayder who was burned at the stake, but rather the Lord of Bones.

129. In the TV series, Vargo Hoat was replaced by Locke. In the books, Locke was a house, not a person.

130. The TV show was so popular that trailers for it began displaying in movie theaters.

131. The books were optioned for TV after the producers finished the Red Wedding chapter in *A Storm of swords.*

132. The actor who played The Mountain (Hafthór Júlíus Björnsson) is the third-strongest man in the world. Investigators determined it is "likely" he would be able to crush a man's skull in real life. In the story however, he doesn't actually crush the Viper's skull. He just punches him so hard his head caves in.

133. All bastard children wear inverted versions of their house colors.

134. The Iron Throne is not seen once on-screen in season 5 of Game of Thrones.

135. One of the animal trainers (Caroline Benoist) died of swine flu during filming of the first season. The episode: *The Wolf and the Lion* was dedicated to her in the credits.

136. In the Battle of Blackwater, Tyrion was only supposed to say "I'll lead the attack." The idea to say it twice, once loudly and once quietly to himself was Peter Dinklage's.

137. After filing his death scene, Sean Bean (Ned Stark) kicked around his fake head with the crew like a soccer ball.

138. In each season of Game of Thrones a king is killed.

139. Only one episode of the TV series takes place in a single location. That location is The Wall.

140. Red hair is rare in Wildling territory and they consider it a sign of very good luck.

141. There was no fight between Mago and Khal Drogo in the books. It was written specifically for the TV show. George RR Martin wrote that episode and it was the first screenplay he had written in 15 years. In the books, Khal Drogo was not even injured by Mago. He was injured by one of Ogo's bloodriders.